387.7

D1520597

January, 2011

Your Government:
How It Works

The Federal Aviation Administration

Andrea Canavan

Chelsea House Publishers
Philadelphia

CHELSEA HOUSE PUBLISHERS
Editor in Chief Sally Cheney
Director of Production Kim Shinners
Creative Manager Takeshi Takahashi
Manufacturing Manager Diann Grasse

Staff for THE FEDERAL AVIATION ADMINISTRATION
Assistant Editor Susan Naab
Production Assistant Jaimie Winkler
Picture Researcher Jaimie Winkler
Series Designers Keith Trego, Takeshi Takahashi
Cover Designer Terry Mallon
Layout 21st Century Publishing and Communications, Inc.

The Chelsea House World Wide Web address is
http://www.chelseahouse.com

First Printing
1 3 5 7 9 8 6 4 2

Library of Congress Cataloging-in-Publication Data

Canavan, Andrea.
    The Federal Aviation Administration / by Andrea Canavan.
        p. cm. — (Your government—how it works)
Includes bibliographical references and index.
Summary: Discusses the history and development of the Federal
Aviation Administration, current issues facing this agency, and
challenges for its future.
    ISBN 0-7910-6795-5
    1. United States. Federal Aviation Administration—Juvenile
literature.   2. Aeronautics, Commercial—Government policy—
United States—Juvenile literature. [1. United States. Federal Aviation
Administration. 2. Aeronautics—Government policy.] I. Title.
II. Series.
HE9803.A35 C36 2002
387.7'0973—dc21
                                                2002000145

Contents

YOUR GOVERNMENT HOW IT WORKS

Introduction

Government: Crises of Confidence

Arthur M. Schlesinger, jr.

FROM THE START, Americans have regarded their government with a mixture of reliance and mistrust. The men who founded the republic understood the importance of government. "If men were angels," observed the 51st Federalist Paper, "no government would be necessary." But men are not angels. Because human beings are subject to wicked as well as to noble impulses, government was deemed essential to assure freedom and order.

The American revolutionaries, however, also knew that government could become a source of injury and oppression. The men who gathered in Philadelphia in 1787 to write the Constitution therefore had two purposes in mind: They wanted to establish a strong central authority and to limit that central authority's capacity to abuse its power.

To prevent the abuse of power, the Founding Fathers wrote two basic principles into the Constitution. The principle of federalism divided power between the state governments and the central authority. The principle of the separation of powers subdivided the central authority itself into three branches—the executive, the legislative, and the judiciary—so that "each may be a check on the other."

YOUR GOVERNMENT: HOW IT WORKS examines some of the major parts of that central authority, the federal government. It explains how various officials, agencies, and departments operate and explores the political

Introduction

organizations that have grown up to serve the needs of government.

The federal government as presented in the Constitution was more an idealistic construct than a practical administrative structure. It was barely functional when it came into being.

This was especially true of the executive branch. The Constitution did not describe the executive branch in any detail. After vesting executive power in the president, it assumed the existence of "executive departments" without specifying what these departments should be. Congress began defining their functions in 1789 by creating the Departments of State, Treasury, and War.

President Washington, assisted by Secretary of the Treasury Alexander Hamilton, equipped the infant republic with a working administrative structure. Congress also continued that process by creating more executive departments as they were needed.

Throughout the 19th century, the number of federal government workers increased at a consistently faster rate than did the population. Increasing concerns about the politicization of public service led to efforts—bitterly opposed by politicians—to reform it in the latter part of the century.

The 20th century saw considerable expansion of the federal establishment. More importantly, it saw growing impatience with bureaucracy in society as a whole.

The Great Depression during the 1930s confronted the nation with its greatest crisis since the Civil War. Under Franklin Roosevelt, the New Deal reshaped the federal government, assigning it a variety of new responsibilities and greatly expanding its regulatory functions. By 1940, the number of federal workers passed the 1 million mark.

Critics complained of big government and bureaucracy. Business owners resented federal regulation. Conservatives worried about the impact of paternalistic government on self-reliance, on community responsibility, and on economic and personal freedom.

When the United States entered World War II in 1941, government agencies focused their energies on supporting the war effort. By the end of World War II, federal civilian employment had risen to 3.8 million. With peace, the federal establishment declined to around 2 million in 1950. Then growth resumed, reaching 2.8 million by the 1980s.

A large part of this growth was the result of the national government assuming new functions such as: affirmative action in civil rights, environmental protection, and safety and health in the workplace.

Some critics became convinced that the national government was a steadily growing behemoth swallowing up the liberties of the people. The 1980s brought new intensity to the debate about government growth. Foes of Washington bureaucrats preferred local government, feeling it more responsive to popular needs.

But local government is characteristically the government of the locally powerful. Historically, the locally powerless have often won their human and constitutional rights by appealing to the national government. The national government has defended racial justice against local bigotry, upheld the Bill of Rights against local vigilantism, and protected natural resources from local greed. It has civilized industry and secured the rights of labor organizations. Had the states' rights creed prevailed, perhaps slavery would still exist in the United States.

Americans are still of two minds. When pollsters ask large, spacious questions—Do you think government has become too involved in your lives? Do you think government should stop regulating business?— a sizable majority opposes big government. But when asked specific questions about the practical work of government—Do you favor Social Security? Unemployment compensation? Medicare? Health and safety standards in factories? Environmental protection?—a sizable majority approves of intervention.

We do not like bureaucracy, but we cannot live without it. We need its genius for organizing the intricate details of our daily lives. Without bureaucracy, modern society would collapse. It would be impossible to run any of the large public and private organizations we depend on without bureaucracy's division of labor and hierarchy of authority. The challenge is to keep these necessary structures of our civilization flexible, efficient, and capable of innovation.

More than 200 years after the drafting of the Constitution, Americans still rely on government but also mistrust it. These attitudes continue to serve us well. What we mistrust, we are more likely to monitor. And government needs our constant attention if it is to avoid inefficiency, incompetence, and arbitrariness. Without our informed participation, it cannot serve us individually or help us as a people to attain the lofty goals of the Founding Fathers.

On September 11, 2001, hijackers flew two planes into the World Trade Center's twin towers. The Pentagon in Washington, D.C. was also attacked.

CHAPTER

1

Safety in the Sky

September 11, 2001

It was an ordinary Tuesday morning in New York City. Workers in the financial district had settled into their jobs. Latecomers were getting coffee. Most of the people in the North Tower of the World Trade Center's twin towers didn't pay attention to the sound of an airplane—until it got very loud and a shadow crossed the windows of the upper floors. Suddenly, the sound reached a deafening roar. Immediately, an earsplitting metallic crash and a tremendous explosion shook the huge 110-story building. Reverberations from the crashed jetliner filled all of Manhattan and beyond. Only minutes later, a similar crash thundered into the morning air. The South Tower was also hit. Within an hour, a third jetliner hit the Pentagon building in Washington, D.C., and, minutes later, a fourth hijacked plane crashed into a field in Pennsylvania, in an aborted attempt to reach the Pentagon. This was a well-planned terrorist attack by hijackers against the United States. The weapons were America's own aircraft. The Federal Aviation Administration (FAA) had a big job on their hands.

AN ESTIMATED 3,000 people died as a result of the attacks, including 500 rescue workers and the passengers on board the doomed flights. America had not seen such devastation on its own soil since 1941, when the attack on Pearl Harbor killed 2,400 Americans.

As soon as it became apparent that the airline attacks were related and might be part of a larger terrorist scheme, the FAA took action. Almost immediately, the FAA instituted a national **lockdown**, thereby halting all flight operations at the nation's airports for the first time in U.S. history. The FAA and the aviation community moved quickly to regain the public's trust and to ensure their safety against future terrorist attacks. While the airlines scrambled to enforce the FAA's new safety regulations, including reinforced **cockpit** doors and strict baggage guidelines, the FAA itself began, among other security measures, recruiting additional **federal air marshals**. In addition, Congress voted to make airport baggage screeners federal employees, resulting in better training and increased pay for those workers. In January 2002, after several minor terrorist incidents, the FAA further tightened air travel security. All carry-on and checked baggage were to be scanned.

December 21, 1988

Excited to return home to their families in time for Christmas, 259 passengers, among them university students, military personnel, business people and members of the flight crew boarded Pan Am Flight 103. A number of passengers had boarded the aircraft on a connecting flight from Frankfurt Main Airport in West Germany to London's Heathrow Airport. The aircraft, a hulking **Boeing 747** jetliner, was scheduled to make a stop at New York's JFK Airport before heading to its final destination in Detroit, Michigan.

As the passengers settled in for their 7½-hour flight and the crew prepared for take-off, everything seemed like business as usual. The pilot went through all the customary procedures for departure and lifted the aircraft off the runway without a problem. About 90 minutes into the flight, the pilot made a routine call to **air traffic control** to identify his flight and confirm that he had reached his cruising **altitude.** Within minutes, the air-traffic controller who had received the call lost sight of Flight 103 on his **radar** screen. He tried repeatedly to contact the pilot but received no answer. His worst fears were confirmed when a supervisor informed him of the tragic news: Pan Am Flight 103 had exploded over the quiet farming village of Lockerbie, Scotland.

Tragically, all 259 passengers on board and 11 people on the ground were killed in the Flight 103 disaster. People everywhere were saddened and outraged. As with any large-scale disaster, everyone wanted answers. What had caused the explosion? A terrorist attack? Mechanical failure? Human error? Americans looked to the FAA for an answer.

Investigating the Lockerbie Crash

The primary mission of the FAA is to provide safe air transportation. When disaster strikes in the air or, as is increasingly the case, on the runway, both the FAA and the National Transportation Safety Board (NTSB) have the responsibility of investigating the crash. However, only the FAA, a United States government body operating under the Department of Transportation (DOT), has the authority to enforce security regulations and standards.

In the case of the Pan Am Flight 103 disaster, an extensive investigation led authorities to determine that a terrorist bomb had caused the explosion. The next step was to determine how a bomb could have been successfully smuggled on board. This immediately brought the issue of airport security to the forefront. It was soon revealed that Pan Am had failed routine security tests recently conducted by both the FAA and Pan Am's own security agency, Alert Management Systems, Inc. In fact, just months before the Flight 103 disaster, the FAA had found flaws in Pan Am's security system at the Frankfurt airport, the same airport where authorities believed the bomb had been smuggled on board with passenger baggage. Many critics blamed the FAA for failing to enforce its own policies and to fine Pan Am for their seriously flawed security system.

Furthermore, it was revealed that the FAA had issued a number of aviation security bulletins to all airlines regarding increased terrorist threats. One of the bulletins, issued nearly two weeks before the Flight 103 disaster, warned all major airlines that an anonymous caller had telephoned a U.S. embassy in Europe stating that sometime within the next two weeks there would be a bombing attempt against a Pan Am aircraft flying from Frankfurt to the United States. Although the FAA receives numerous, usually meaningless, warnings of terrorist activity, the administration took the threat seriously enough to issue a security bulletin, which was not released to the general public. It was later discovered that the memo did not reach any security personnel at the Frankfurt airport. According to Pan Am officials, security was increased after the airline received the FAA advisory.

In the midst of all the finger pointing, the FAA was quick to install stricter security measures only a week after the Flight 103 disaster had occurred. Directed at U.S. carriers at all airports in Europe and the Middle East, the safety measures required that the airlines physically search or x-ray all checked baggage, conduct additional random checks of passengers and baggage, and check that all baggage loaded onto an international flight belongs to a passenger on that flight.

Pan Am Flight 103's crash left a deep crater in the ground, in addition to destroying houses in the town of Lockerbie, Scotland.

Port of Portland

Above travelers at the Portland International Airport in Portland, Oregon on November 21, 2001. New security measures have been installed since the September 11, 2001 attacks on the World Trade Center and the Pentagon. Passengers are asked to arrive up to two hours before departure to allow ample time for new security inspection procedures.

Yet an unannounced FAA inspection at Frankfurt airport almost one year after the Lockerbie incident, revealed that many of Pan Am's security problems persisted. Finally, after repeated warnings and pressure from the FAA and other agencies, Pan Am was able to correct its security problems and pass inspection. The FAA fined Pan Am $630,000 for security violations that occurred before and after the Flight 103 incident.

Although critics are quick to blame the FAA for not taking adequate preventive measures and for reacting only in the face of tragedy, no amount of FAA intervention will provide for fail-safe aviation. As air-safety expert Rudolph Kapustin commented after a ValuJet tragedy that killed 109 passengers in the Everglades in Florida in May 1996, "We are dealing with machines and people, and they are not flawless. Sadly, we're going to have accidents. But we can have fewer accidents." Consequently, in contrast to media overexposure that might lead you to believe otherwise, flying on a U.S. airline remains one of the safest ways to travel in the world.

FAA Responsibilities

The FAA has a bulk of other responsibilities under its wing beyond that of acting as watchdog for both the domestic and foreign airlines. And, as reported in a Time Magazine article in 1996, "the FAA is financially strapped, and has lost 5,000 employees since 1993. It has a constant shortage of inspectors, and rather than inspecting, they must devote increasing amounts of time to clerical tasks."

Because of the FAA's heavy reliance on the **Aviation Trust Fund**, the federal government has been able to make large Congressional cuts to the FAA's already slim federal budget. While such cuts have resulted in more aid for other federal programs, the already struggling FAA has had even fewer funds to contend with. Working under budget and understaffed, the FAA recognizes its responsibilities as such:

• *Safety Regulation*: Issuing and enforcing regulations and standards relating to the manufacture, operation, and maintenance of aircraft; certifying and rating pilots and airports; enforcing regulations under the Hazardous Materials Transportation Act.

• *Airspace and Air Traffic Management*: Operating a network of airport towers, air route traffic control centers, and flight service stations; developing air traffic rules; allocating the use of airspace; providing security control of air traffic to meet national defense requirements.

• *Air Navigation Facilities*: Constructing or installing visual and electronic aids to air navigation; maintaining, operating and assuring the quality of air navigation facilities.

• *Civil Aviation Abroad*: Promoting **civil aviation** abroad (as mandated by legislation); exchanging aeronautical information with foreign authorities; certifying foreign repair shops, airmen, and mechanics; providing technical assistance and training; negotiating "airworthiness" agreements; providing technical representation at international conferences.

• *Commercial Space Transportation*: Regulating and encouraging the U.S. commercial space transportation industry; providing licenses to commercial space launch facilities.

• *Research, Engineering, and Development*: Engaging in research, engineering, and development aimed at providing maximum security and efficiency of air navigation and air traffic control; performing **aeromedical** research and supporting development of improved aircraft, engines, and equipment; conducting tests and evaluations of aviation systems, devices, materials, procedures, and other things.

• *Additional Programs*: Providing a system for registering aircraft; administering an aviation insurance program; developing specifications for aeronautical charts; developing and implementing programs to control aircraft noise and other environmental effects of civil aviation; publishing information on airways, airport services and technical subjects relating to **aeronautics.**

The Aeronautics Branch of the Department of Commerce was created on May 20, 1926. This gave birth to the formally established Federal Aviation Agency by the Federal Aviation Act of 1958. The FAA as it exists today began its current incarnation on April 1, 1967, when it began operating as one of the organizations under the newly created Department of Transportation.

Much has changed since the establishment of aviation regulation in the 1920s, in terms of both aeronautical technology and safety concerns. While mechanical and structural safety concerns have existed since the first operational aircraft took flight, new safety issues have arisen to challenge the aviation industry and expand the scope of the FAA's responsibilities.

In the 1970s, the aviation industry was plagued by the new threat of airline **hijacking.** The 1980s witnessed the modern era of air terrorism. The 1990s saw an increase in air and runway collisions due to the rapid increase of air traffic. To date, the most devastating blow to the aviation industry, and to America at large, occurred on the morning of September 11, 2001.

To the horror of the world, the first of the two World Trade Center buildings crumbles to the ground after two planes, which had been hijacked by terrorists, crashed into them on September 11, 2001.

This photograph documents one of the early airplanes constructed by Orville and Wilbur Wright. Here, they are demonstrating one of their first airplanes on an airfield in Le Mans, France.

CHAPTER 2

Early Aviation

THROUGHOUT TIME, HUMANKIND has been fascinated by the prospect of flight. By first studying the flight of birds, many innovative thinkers, including artist Leonardo da Vinci, have proposed a myriad of devices that might allow humans to take to the skies. Although various forms of crude aviation—gliders, hot-air balloons, **dirigibles**—have taken form throughout history, the world's first successful flight in a powered, heavier-than-air craft did not occur until the beginning of the 20th century.

On a windy morning in December 17, 1903, just outside Kitty Hawk, North Carolina, brothers Orville and Wilbur Wright decided to test their new flying machine, later known as *Flyer I*. Despite the harsh weather conditions, *Flyer I* remained in the air for 12 seconds, marking the first ever sustained, piloted flight. Later that day, the brothers were able to break their own record, by sustaining flight for 59 seconds.

Despite the obvious historical significance of the Wrights' accomplishments, the news of *Flyer I* caused surprisingly little stir among a skeptical press and public, who had been duped by similar news in the past. In fact, it was not until 1908, when Wilbur traveled to Europe and completed a masterful flight of approximately 2 hours and 20 minutes that the Wrights were properly recognized for their groundbreaking achievements.

The Wrights' aeronautical advances marked the beginning of huge developments in aviation, for the brothers themselves and for innovators worldwide. In fact, by 1909, despite increased developments by the Wright brothers and other American innovators, such as plane designer Glenn Curtiss, America no longer dominated the field of aviation. The Europeans, and especially the French, were quick to pick up where the Americans left off, primarily because they had access to funds that American aviators did not. By 1914, the French alone had spent more than $35 million on aviation, whereas the U.S. government had allotted only $685,000 to such endeavors.

In the years leading to **World War I** (1914-1918), American pilots, designers and innovators continued to make considerable improvements to the field of aviation. By 1911, American aviator Calbraith P. Rodgers made the first transcontinental flight, from New York City to Long Beach, California. That same year, the U.S. Post Office Department approved the transportation of mail by airplane, although it lasted only a week and was not reinstated until 1918 with an experimental airmail service between New York City and Washington, D.C.

Military and Postal Carriers

Not until the start of World War I in 1914 did the world witness a tremendous surge in aviation development, primarily in the realm of **military aviation**. Motivated by the pressure of war, aircraft designers scrambled to develop aircraft suited to specialized military purposes including **reconnaissance**, attack, and bombing. The possibility of a war occurring in both the sky and the trenches also meant that more pilots needed to be trained—and fast. It so happened that more pilots were trained and more planes were built during the four years of conflict than in the 13 years since the first flight.

At the start of the war, unarmed airplanes had been used primarily for surveying enemy territory and activities, with pilots from opposing sides even offering a friendly wave as they flew past each other. However, it was not long before airplanes had been transformed largely into weapons of aerial warfare, with Germany gaining dominance at the outset of the war. The allies were quick to respond with new designs, and by 1916, the Allies were a viable challenge to Germany's reign of the skies. Not until the entrance of U.S. forces in 1917 did the Allied forces become close to gaining air supremacy. In fact, as the war neared an end in 1918, the U.S. Air Service led the largest attack force of planes that the war had seen when it pummeled Germany with a brigade of 1,500 fighter and bomber planes.

Although impressive technological advances had been made on both sides of the Atlantic during World War I, the field of aviation remained immature and relatively unregulated. In America, however, it would not be long before the federal government stepped in. The first major developments in civil aviation were primarily made within the U.S. Post Office Department. Having obtained a number of surplus warplanes and encouraged by earlier ventures, the Post Office Department established a number of transcontinental airmail routes in 1919 and 1920. However, because there were no lighted airfields or flashing beacons, pilots could not navigate after dark. The mail had to be transferred to trains at night. It was not until 1924 that a system of radio beacons was installed coast-to-coast to facilitate airmail service during the day and night.

Despite these developments, the aviation industry still

One of the earlier uses of airplanes was to transport mail. The postal airplane pictured here was used in Sydney, Australia for Adelaide Aerial Mail in 1925.

needed a major boost to reach any kind of commercial or economic significance. First off, there was relatively little demand for air travel in the United States after World War I. While many of Europe's ground transportation systems had been destroyed by the war, trains in the United States were functioning with more speed and reliability than airplanes. However, pilots were exploring new ways to turn aviation into a profitable field. Even before World War I, a number of daring pilots had found ways to exploit the commercial potential of airplanes by engaging in for-profit activities such as **barnstorming**, air racing, and aerial photography.

However, business people and bankers remained wary of investing in what they viewed to be an unsafe and under-regulated venture. Aviation leaders echoed this belief back to a reluctant Congress, declaring that the airplane could not possibly reach its full commercial potential without feder-ally regulated safety standards. While the Post Office did impose regulations on its pilots, requiring at least 500 hours of flight time, a qualifying and medical exam and plane inspections, the industry was still too unstable to appear profitable. Most airfields remained unpaved and unmarked; many of the airplanes had no centralized weather service, air-to-ground radio service, or aerial maps. Becoming an airmail pilot was risky enough, but investing in a fledgling industry was too risky for most businesspeople to seriously consider. By 1925, only 9 of the 40 pilots hired by the Post Office in 1918 had survived.

Government Regulation Begins

Even by 1924, with Europe already offering air-passenger services and government regulation, the United States had failed at its few attempts to establish a successful passenger airline. However, the sluggishness of air commerce slowly began reversing itself. This was due in part to renewed federal interest and the unsolicited promotion of aviation by American **ace** pilots such as Charles A. Lindbergh and Eddie Rickenbacker. While the world's first nonstop transatlantic flight had been made by two British aviators in 1919, Lindbergh, a former airmail pilot, made the first nonstop flight alone across the Atlantic Ocean in 1927, traveling form New York to Paris in 33.5 hours.

Unlike any other industry in America's past, the members of the aviation community practically begged Congress to put the aviation industry completely under federal control. Pro-regulators like Orville Wright recognized that in addition to safety regulation, the government needed to provide for the development of airways and airports, just as it subsidized necessary developments for competing forms of transport—the shipping, railroad, and motor vehicle industries. In addition to the debate over government regulation of aviation in general, another debate raged in Congress regarding the unification or separation of civil and military aviation.

Congress soon caved in to the increased public outcry

Charles Lindbergh was a famous pilot in the 1920s. Once an airmail pilot, he eventually set a new record when he was the first man to fly alone nonstop across the Atlantic Ocean. His historic flight took him from New York to Paris in 33.5 hours; today this same flight lasts a mere 7 hours.

and discord within the aviation community. While still hesitant to assume the financial obligation that would coincide with government regulation, Congress took the first step toward regulation and the separation of civil and military aviation. Congress passed the Kelly Air Mail Act in 1925. The first of many legislative acts within the industry, the Kelly Act authorized the Post Office Department to contract with private contractors for the air delivery of U.S. mail. After amended legislation the following year, 14 domestic airmail lines were established, and additional lines were extended between the United States and Central and

South America and between the United States and Canada.

The following year proved pivotal for the aviation industry. On May 20, 1926, President Calvin Coolidge (1923-1929) signed the Air Commerce Act of 1926, thereby marking the beginning of government regulation of the airways and paving the way for the FAA as we know it today. Under the authorization of the new law, an Aeronautics Branch was created within the Department of Commerce and included the appointment of assistant secretaries for air in the Navy, Army, and Commerce Department. Secretary of Commerce Herbert Hoover (and later President Hoover from 1929 to 1933) appointed William P. McCracken, Jr., a former army pilot and long-time advocate of federal regulation of civil aviation, to the position of Assistant Secretary of Commerce for Aeronautics. McCracken's list of duties included:

- Promoting air commerce

- Designating and establishing airways

- Establishing and operating aids to air navigation

- Licensing pilots

- Issuing airworthiness certificates to aircrafts

- Imposing penalties for air-safety violations

- Investigating aircraft accidents

Operating on a meager fiscal budget during its first year, the Aeronautics Branch initially split its responsibilities with other federal agencies. The Aeronautical Research Division of the Bureau of Standards provided research and development, the Lighthouse Service assumed responsibility for navigational aids and the Coast and Geodetic Survey provided for an airway mapping service. The Air Commerce Act left the responsibility of airport construction and maintenance to local authorities. The federal government viewed airport development to be too costly a proposition and likened airports to shipping docks, which had always been funded by private and municipal investments. By 1928, emergency landing fields, air-to-ground communication systems, and beacon-lighted airways had been established.

Because of these new regulations and standards, interest in the commercial viability of the airplane increased dramatically. Finally, U.S. investors were willing to take a chance on what was to become a lucrative enterprise for early airlines. The combination of government funds, increased safety measures, and the well-publicized feats of famous aviators all contributed to what would become a flourishing industry.

While competing for government airmail contracts, several new airline companies also began exploring the profitability of passenger transport services in the mid to late 1920s. In fact, many of the current major U.S. airlines, such as Pan Am, TWA, and American, descend from the early mail carriers. While the first international passenger service—between Key West, Florida, and Havana, Cuba—had been introduced in 1920, its profitability proved short lived. In fact, the lure of lucrative airmail contracts overshadowed that of passenger service throughout the 1920s. Not until the mid 1930s, when new designs for passenger planes began emerging, did passenger service again become profitable.

One of the most popular passenger plane models, the Ford Trimotor, also known as the "Tin Goose," was produced by the Ford Motor Company in 1927. Another important aircraft, the DC-3, produced by the Douglas Aircraft Company in 1936, revolutionized passenger comfort and is credited as the first plane to make passenger airlines profitable. The DC-3 seated 21 passengers, whereas earlier aircraft had been able to seat between 8 and 16 passengers. And the DC-3 was able to travel coast-to-coast in the United States in 16 hours—a short trip by the standards of the1930s.

By this time, **commercial aviation** had proved to be a profitable and expansive enterprise. As airplanes themselves

In the days before air travel become commonplace, light-houses were crucial to air safety. The St. George Reef Lighthouse, located off the coast of Crescent City, California, is 104 years old. It is in the process of being restored by the state.

had become more comfortable and dependable, long-distance and transoceanic flights had become more frequent. Whereas airmail service had once seemed the only money-making possibility within the commercial aviation industry, passenger and **cargo** services had become equally lucrative. Revolutionary new airplane designs had also opened up nearly a dozen new business opportunities—from writing ads in the sky to spraying fields with insecticides. All of the growth and development within the commercial aviation industry required that the federal government soon reconsider its role in air safety and regulation.

Long before the days of luxurious private jets, the man who would be elected the 32d president of the United States, Franklin Delano Roosevelt, had his own airplane. Here he is being flown to accept the Democratic nomination for president in 1932.

CHAPTER 3

Early Regulation: The Civil Aeronautics Authority

WHEN PRESIDENT FRANKLIN D. Roosevelt (1933-1945) came into office, America was still in the midst of the **Great Depression**. As a result, some government agencies suffered cutbacks to their federal funds. The Aeronautics Branch was among them. Consequently, despite all the progress that the Aeronautics Branch had made, air safety suffered greatly.

In 1935, an airplane crash killed Senator Bronson M. Cutting of New Mexico. This tragedy finally prompted Congress to reexamine its financial obligation to air safety as well as its role in the investigation of airplane accidents. As a result of the follow-up investigation, Congress allocated more funds for the promotion of air safety and placed the three major air traffic control towers under federal jurisdiction.

Civil Aeronautics Act

Congress passed the Civil Aeronautics Act of 1938, enacting new air safety legislation. The Civil Aeronautics Act, which later underwent numerous amendments, removed aviation control from the Department of Commerce and instead established an independent new agency, the Civil Aeronautics Authority (CAA). By this time, President Roosevelt had long been expressing a desire for a unified and independent agency to regulate the aviation industry. In 1935, he had communicated his views to Congress, stating, "Air transportation should be brought into a proper relation to other forms of transportation by subjecting it to regulation by the same agency."

The CAA was Roosevelt's answer, a new federal agency designed to keep its functions as an agent of Congress separate from its functions as an agent of the president. The CAA comprised three elements:

1. The Civil Aeronautics Authority (the same name as the agency as a whole), a five-person commission that would perform legislative and judicial functions as related to safety and economic regulation

2. The Air Safety Board, a three-person entity operating independently within the agency and responsible for investigating airplane accidents

3. The Administrator of the Authority, operating independently of the five-person authority and responsible for executive and operational functions within the agency, such as promoting civil aeronautics and commerce, establishing and improving civil airways and navigation facilities, and regulating air traffic

In 1939, President Roosevelt signed the Civilian Pilot Training Act into law; the legislation authorized the CAA to conduct programs at educational institutions for the training of civilian pilots and as preparation for private pilot certification. The act, which specified, "none of the benefits of training or programs shall be denied on account of race, creed, or color," proved to be an important development for African-Americans in aviation. Although African-American aviators had been active in the years preceding World War I—a time when nearly all pilots were unlicensed—James Herman Banning is recognized as the first African-American pilot to receive a federal pilot license in 1928.

In spite of various developments and programs managed by the CAA in its first year, the agency was soon being criticized for its size and large appropriation of funds (at the time, the agency was one of the largest in the government, with nearly 3,000 employees and funds exceeding $14 million). Both President Roosevelt and Congress recognized that a reorganization of the agency was in order. Thus, under the direction of President Roosevelt, the Bureau of the Budget began a study of the organization of the CAA.

Following the recommendations of the Bureau of the Budget, President Roosevelt issued two executive orders in 1940 that resulted in a new division of aviation responsibilities:

- The five-member authority was transferred to the Department of Commerce and renamed the Civil Aeronautics Board (CAB)

- The Air Safety Board was abolished, and its accident-investigating functions were assigned to the new Civil Aeronautics Board.

- The Administrator, whose functions now included all safety regulation except rulemaking and the power to suspend or revoke certificates, was renamed the Administrator of Civil Aeronautics and was also transferred to the Department of Commerce. In addition, 18 units reported directly to the Administrator: the Management Planning Section; the Personnel Section; Washington National Airport; the Federal Airways Service; the Certificate and Inspection Division; the Civilian Pilot Training Division; the Legal (Compliance) Division; the Aviation Medical Division; the Information and Statistics Division; the Administrative Division; a Coordinator of Field Activities; and the seven regional managers.

Around this time, **World War II** (1939–1945) had already broken out in Central Europe, and aircraft again became the focus of accelerated development worldwide. Important advances were achieved in the speed and efficiency of the fighter and bomber planes of World War II, as well as planes used to transport parachute troops and tanks. Whereas World War I had ushered in the advent of air combat, the Second World War resulted in a deadlier form of aerial warfare—the atomic bomb.

The aviation industry in the United States had been producing planes at an increased rate even before the United States entered World War II. Large orders from France and Britain at the start of the war kept the airline production lines rapidly churning out planes. In 1939, for example, 2,200 military aircraft were produced. By 1944, when the United States was fully immersed in the war, production topped at nearly 100,000 planes. In total, the government spent an estimated $45 billion on aircraft for the war.

The United States entered the war on December 8, 1941, one day after Japanese bombers surprise-attacked American Navy planes at their base in Pearl Harbor, Hawaii. On December 11, Germany and Italy declared war on the United States. As the United States entered the Second World War, President Roosevelt was quick to transform the nation's aviation industry into an agent of national defense. First, he ordered the transformation of the Civilian Pilot Training Program into a wartime program. Private operators subsequently expanded their facilities and trained thousands of students to become military pilots. In addition, a number of aircraft that had been designed for passenger use were instead put to use in the military.

Next, Roosevelt directed the Secretary of Commerce "to exercise his control and jurisdiction over civil aviation in accordance with requirements for the successful prosecution of the war, as may be requested by the Secretary of War." The Executive order also authorized the Secretary of War to "take possession and assume control of any civil aviation system, or systems, or any part thereof, to the extent necessary for the successful prosecution of the war." Consequently, the Secretary of War immediately requested that long-range CAA projects for commissioning air-route traffic control centers "be expedited to the fullest extent possible in the interest of National Defense." Within a few months, the CAA had established seven new air-route traffic control centers and was working to complete its planned communications network, which would include an expanded flight advisory service and a flight communications service.

During 1941, American military aircraft were in action on all fronts. As part of the national defense effort, the CAA launched its first Inter-American Aviation Training Program in 1941. By the end of the fourth program, 894 Latin-Americans had received training in aeronautical sciences. The number of persons employed in the aviation industry totaled 450,000, compared with about 193,000 employed before World War II.

Women Pilots

Although female pilots had been flying and performing daring feats since the early 20th century (Harriet Quimby was the first woman to receive a pilot's license in 1911; Amelia Earhart was the first woman to fly alone across the Atlantic Ocean in 1932), the aviation industry remained skeptical about female pilots. In fact, as late as the 1940s, women could find employment within the aviation industry *only* by working as stewardesses, as flight attendants were then called. Attitudes about women pilots began to change, however, as the world became engulfed in the Second World War, and

Early in the era of aviation, Harriet Quimbly (1875-1912) was a pioneer, being the first woman to obtain a pilot's license. Women would not be able to find employment in aviation outside of a flight attendant career until the early 1940s.

World War II brought a new chapter to the history of aviation. This U.S. marine spotter plane flew over Okinawa, Japan on June 2, 1945. The smoke comes from artillery and mortar fired on enemy strongholds.

the shortage of trained male pilots became apparent. Although women pilots had been accepted into Britain's Air Transport Auxiliary (ATA) in 1940, the Air Transport Auxiliary began accepting American women on a trial basis in 1941; American racing pilot Jackie Cochran, who had served with the Air Transport Auxiliary, founded the U.S. Women's Airforce Service Pilots (WASPs) in 1942.

Faster Planes

As airplane production reached its peak toward the end of the war, both the Allies and the Germans were experimenting with turbojet engines—exhaust-driven engines that allowed aircraft to fly at extremely high speeds. Spurred by military interest, experimentation with new designs, metals, and technology led to the development of turbojet- and rocket-powered airplanes. Consequently, passenger transport was again revolutionized, leading to such developments as pressurized cabins and, eventually, **supersonic transport**.

After World War II, the production of military aircraft in the United States was significantly reduced, whereas civilian aircraft orders increased considerably. Advances in the size and speed of aircraft, as well as CAA-managed improvements to airports, communications services (especially weather reporting and forecasting), and navigational aid networks, resulted in a surge of public demand for air transportation. Aircraft developments during World War II also led to a boom in corporate aviation. After the war, a number of military aircraft were converted into airplanes used solely for the transportation of corporate executives.

An Overburdened CAA

Although regulatory efforts improved during the post-war boom in aviation, the issue of large-scale international air travel needed to be addressed. The issue had been addressed at conferences in the past, most notably at the International Civil Aviation Conference held in Chicago in 1944, which was attended by representatives from 52 countries. As a result of the conference, an agreement known as the "Chicago Convention" was drafted, thereby laying the groundwork for the first global organization for civil aviation, the International Civil Aviation Organization (ICAO). This organization, created in 1947, still exists today and seeks to ensure the safe development of aviation worldwide.

However, by the 1950s, the United States government could no longer ignore the fact that the CAA was unable to adequately address its own domestic aviation concerns. Despite all of the progress initiated by the CAA in the post-war years (such as the use of mandatory flight recorders on aircrafts and, increasingly, radar-equipped control towers), the agency was now under-funded and overburdened. In addition to its financial struggles, the CAA faced a bulk of new challenges, ranging from airport zoning disputes and noise pollution to increased congestion on the runways.

By the time passenger jets were in service in the mid 1950s, divided air traffic control responsibilities within the CAA made it impossible for the agency to effectively regulate the aviation industry. Despite the obvious need for a makeover of the CAA, Congress was not moved to action until a deadly mid-air collision occurred in 1956. When subsequent Congressional hearings revealed numerous problems within air traffic control, the need for an independent federal aviation agency could no longer be overlooked.

The Boeing 747 jumbo jet is the largest commercial aircraft in use today. Taking off for the first time on February 9, 1969, the Boeing 747 can carry 400 passengers and is powered by four jet engines.

CHAPTER 4

The Federal Aviation Administration is Born

UNDER THE DIRECTION of President Dwight D. Eisenhower (1953-1961), two air force generals, General Elwood Quesada and General Edward P. Curtis, designed a proposal for the creation of a new federal agency that would supersede the CAA. In 1957, President Eisenhower signed the Airways Modernization Act, which established an interim organization until an independent aviation authority could be created. The interim organization, the Airways Modernization Board, was assigned the task of selecting systems, procedures, and devices that would promote maximum coordination of air traffic control and air defense systems; General Quesada was selected as chairman of the Airways Modernization Board.

The following year, Eisenhower signed the Federal Aviation Act of 1958. The new legislation repealed the Air Commerce Act of 1926, the Civil Aeronautics Act of 1938, and the Airways Modernization Act of 1957. The various functions initially assigned by the repealed laws were split between two agencies that would function independently of the Department of Commerce—the newly created Federal Aviation Administration (FAA), renamed from Federal Aviation Agency, and the preexisting Civil Aeronautics Board.

With General Quesada serving as administrator, the FAA first took over the responsibilities and personnel of the Airways Modernization Board and eventually inherited the core organization and functions of the CAA. The Federal Aviation Act clearly stated the powers and regulations of the Administrator as follows:

(a) The regulation of air commerce in such manner as to best promote its development and safety and fulfill the requirements of national defense;

(b) The promotion, encouragement, and development of civil aeronautics;

(c) The control of the use of the navigable airspace of the United States and the regulation of both civil and military operations in such airspace in the interest of the safety and efficiency of both;

(d) The consolidation of research and development with respect to air navigation facilities, as well as the installation and operation thereof;

(e) The development and operation of a common system of air traffic control and navigation for both military and civil aircraft."

Pursuant to the act, the Civil Aeronautics Board retained responsibility for the economic regulation of air carriers and accident investigation, whereas safety regulation and enforcement responsibilities were transferred to the FAA. Although the FAA could participate in accident investigation, the Civil Aeronautics Board was solely responsible for the determination of probable cause. This separation of accident investigation and regulatory functions continues within the aviation industry today.

While military officials had always been resistant to the idea of civilian control over military air traffic, the Federal Aviation Act granted the FAA control of both military and civil air traffic. To allay the fears of the military, the act included a provision stating that the military would play an important role in the agency. Furthermore, a military officer could serve as deputy administrator to the FAA, as long as the officer was not on active duty.

That same year, President Eisenhower settled another issue regarding military or civilian control when he signed the National Aeronautics and Space Act of 1958. The act established a single agency, the National Aeronautics and Space Administration (NASA), which would absorb all prior civil and military space organizations relating to space exploration. Although the National Advisory Committee for Aeronautics (NACA) had been functioning since 1915, the issue of space exploration was brought to the forefront by the so-called "space race" occurring between the United States and the former Union of Soviet Socialist Republics (U.S.S.R.), now known as Russia. In this space race, both countries sought to create a rocket that could ultimately reach the moon. Soviet scientists had taken a huge leap forward when they launched Sputnik 1 into orbit around Earth in 1957.

Although NASA is usually the organization responsible for researching aircraft technology, the FAA spearheaded the effort in the mid 1960s to develop a new supersonic transport. Although supersonic jet fighters and bombers had already been introduced in the years following the Second World War, a supersonic aircraft designed for commercial use had yet to be developed. Seeking to fulfill the responsibility of promoting civil aeronautics, the FAA, then headed by General William McKee, sought to design a supersonic transport plane that would encourage air travel. Supersonic aircraft typically

The Soviets started the so-called "space race" when Yuri Gagarin made man's first orbit around Earth on April 21, 1961. He was twenty-seven years old at the time.

encounter less turbulence and aerodynamic drag than aircraft flying within the sound barrier, thereby enabling them to reach speeds above 760 miles per hour (the speed of sound).

While Britain and France worked together to develop a supersonic transport that could fly at twice the speed of sound, the FAA stumbled through its own supersonic transport program. At the time, because of severe oil shortages and the large amount of fuel required by such an aircraft, in addition to environmental concerns over sonic boom and air pollution, the FAA was unable to produce a commercially

useful plane. In 1969, 14 years after first investing in the project, the British and French introduced the world's only supersonic transport plane, the Concorde—capable of carrying 100 passengers and twice surpassing the speed of sound. The United States had entered the race too late and with too little funding. In 1971, President Richard Nixon (1969-1974) cut off all funding for the supersonic transport program, and the FAA was forced to abandon the project.

During the mid 1960s, a number of consumer groups became increasingly vocal about the need for major safety reform within all transportation industries. As a result, President Lyndon B. Johnson (1963-1969) signed the Department of Transportation Act in 1966, which brought previously dispersed transportation functions and agencies, including the FAA, under the wing of one department. The resulting DOT, which began operations in April 1967, would serve as an executive department of the federal government with the purpose of coordinating safe, efficient, and progressive transportation in the United States.

As a result of the act, the Federal Aviation Administration

The legendary Concorde supersonic jet can carry 100 passengers and travels at twice the speed of sound. All Concorde flights were suspended, however, immediately following a crash of one of the Concorde fleet in Paris in 2000, which killed 113 British Airways passengers. More than a year later, Concorde flights resumed on October 22, 2001.

lost its status as an independent agency and was among those agencies transferred to the Department of Transportation. The act also created the five-member NTSB to operate within the new department. In the exercise of its duties, the board was made independent of the secretary of the Department of Transportation, as well as other offices and officers within the department. The National Transportation Safety Board was assigned the following responsibilities:

- Determining the cause or probable cause of transportation accidents

- Reporting the facts, conditions, and circumstances relating to investigated accidents

- Reviewing on appeal the suspension or denial of any certificate or license issued by the secretary of the department or by an administrator.

Air Terrorism

The newly organized FAA prepared to tackle a new challenge—airplane hijacking—and created the Sky Marshal Program in 1968. After 1970, airplane hijackings in the United Stares became a serious problem when Cuban exiles, among others, executed a steady wave of hijackings. In addition to recruiting and training sky marshals, the government signed several international agreements in the 1970s, including one with Cuba, in a concerted attempt to stop hijacking. In 1985, the program was modified and renamed the Federal Air Marshal Program, which is still in existence today. The current program was created shortly after Lebanese Muslims hijacked TWA Flight 847 in demand for the release of Muslim prisoners held by Israel; during the confrontation, which lasted two weeks, the hijackers released 155 hostages (including 39 Americans) in stages and murdered one passenger, a U.S. Navy diver.

4339

Deregulation

Another major change to the aviation industry occurred in the late 1970s when President Jimmy Carter (1977-1981) signed the Airline **Deregulation** Act of 1978. Essentially, the act resulted in a decrease in airline economic regulation (a function of the Civil Aeronautics Board since the Federal Aviation Act of 1958) and therefore an increase in competition. Specifically, the act allowed airlines to dramatically reduce their fares without board approval and allowed new airlines to automatically enter into routes not already protected by other airlines. The Civil Aeronautics Board's authority over fares, routes, and mergers was eventually phased out by 1983. When the Civil Aeronautics Board was completely abolished in December 1984, the National Transportation Safety Board assumed the duty of investigating aviation accidents.

As a result of the act, the number of airlines serving the United States has dramatically increased, whereas airfares have continued to decrease. However, deregulation has also resulted in a number of negative side effects, such as over-burdened air traffic control at major airports and an increase in noise and air pollution.

On June 19, 1985 Shiite Moslem terrorists hijacked a TWA flight from Athens to Rome carrying 155 hostages. The hijackers demanded that 700 Lebanese jailed in Israel be released. The hostages were held for two weeks. One American passenger, a U.S. Navy diver, was killed. As a result of this hijacking, the Sky Marshal Program, instituted in 1968, was transformed into the Federal Air Marshal Program.

The FAA orders a press conference on Thursday December 14, 1995. From right to left: Randy Babbit, president of the American Airline Pilots Association; Federico Pena, National Transportation Secretary; and David Hinson, FAA Administrator, announce new safety rules that seek to hold small commuter planes to the same standards as major air carriers.

CHAPTER 5

Inside the Federal Aviation Administration

AS THE FAA made the transition from agency to administration in the late 1960s with new responsibilities, there was a shift in the types of employees the FAA began to hire. Although the FAA admittedly has a long history of labor-relations problems, it was not until 1968 that the issue reached a boiling point. Before the late 1960s, most FAA employees consisted of former military controllers. However, as the field of aviation expanded, the FAA was forced to choose from a pool of inexperienced candidates. As a result, the FAA began hiring people with minimal aviation background and, in some cases, hiring people with no aviation background at all. To become certified by the FAA, controllers today must complete a set of screening examinations and training courses. After being employed by the FAA, the controllers are sent to its training facility for a 15-week training program. New controllers are required to complete between one and three years of on-the-job training before working independently.

Birth and Death of an Air Traffic Controllers' Union

In January 1968, a group of dissatisfied air traffic controllers in New York voted to create a labor union and formed the Professional Air Traffic Controllers Organization (PATCO). By the end of June 1968, PATCO had a national membership of over 5,000 FAA employees. (Almost 20,000 air traffic controllers, who account for over a third of the FAA staff, are *currently* employed in the United States.) Almost immediately, PATCO made a number of demands to the FAA, including higher pay, early retirement, and other benefits for controllers. After the first of many future quarrels with the FAA, 477 dissatisfied PATCO members staged a "sickout" protest in June 1969, by claiming illness and refusing to report for work. Although the protest lasted only a few days, it affected numerous FAA facilities and resulted in widespread flight delays. Nevertheless, the sickout was less disruptive than the larger protests that followed unsuccessful negotiations between PATCO and the FAA in the 1970s and 1980s.

After a 17-day PATCO sickout in 1970, the Department of Transportation described the actions of PATCO members as a strike against the U.S. government and therefore illegal. As a result, the government obtained temporary restraining orders against PATCO. During a subsequent hearing on the matter, PATCO agreed to call off the sickout; nonetheless, the FAA suspended nearly 1,000 controllers and fired 52 for their role in the strike. During the mid to late 1970s, a number of contracts and agreements were made between PATCO and the FAA, but PATCO continued to demand better

terms and continuously threatened and implemented work "slowdowns."

In April 1981, after 37 negotiating sessions with the FAA, PATCO representatives walked out of contract talks regarding PATCO's proposals for a shorter work-week, early retirement, and increased pay, among other things. PATCO president Robert Poli was quoted by newspapers as stating, "the skies will be silent" if FAA's negotiators do not "come to their senses." Nearly five months later, Poli proved to be true to his word.

On the morning of August 3, 1981—after 11 hours of failed negotiations with the FAA—approx-imately 12,000 members of the 15,000-member PATCO engaged in an illegal strike. As a result, almost half of the nation's daily commercial flights

A labor strike of the Professional Air Traffic Controllers Organization (PATCO) occurred on August 3, 1981. The PATCO members wanted shorter work weeks, early retirement, and other benefits extended to them. As a result of their strike, half of all commercial flights were unable to take off.

had to be grounded. Within hours of the strike, President Ronald Reagan (1981-1989) held an impromptu news conference in which he ordered the strikers to return to work within 48 hours or face permanent dismissal. Approximately 11,000 strikers rejected the ultimatum and were subsequently fired. The union itself had to face enormous fines imposed by the district court of Washington, D.C.

The federal government went even further in imposing disciplinary action against the union. In a series of legal steps, the government worked to seize PATCO's $3.5 million strike fund, to file criminal complaints against PATCO officials, and to issue restraining orders against the strikers. In less than a year, PATCO faced a $40 million debt. In July 1982, PATCO President Gary Eads filed for bankruptcy, declaring, "It is over for PATCO. The union is gone."

PATCO was not the only organization to suffer casualties in the aftermath of the strike. Because of a post-strike ban on re-employment, the number of air traffic controllers employed by the FAA after the strike decreased to approximately 4,200 from nearly 16,500 controllers before the strike. Although military controllers stepped in to assume air traffic responsibilities after the strike, the air traffic control system never fully recovered from the significant loss of employees. In 1987, the controllers began raising concerns similar to those of PATCO and formed a new union, the National Air Traffic Controllers Association (NATCA).

Owing to unsuccessful attempts by Congress to lift Reagan's re-employment ban throughout the 1980s, the FAA often met the controller shortage at the expense of the flying public. Flights were frequently delayed, sometimes for hours, while controllers held aircraft on the ground until the system could safely accommodate them. Not until the 1990s, with the completion of a major FAA training program and the lifting of the re-employment ban, was the FAA again able to adequately address air traffic control.

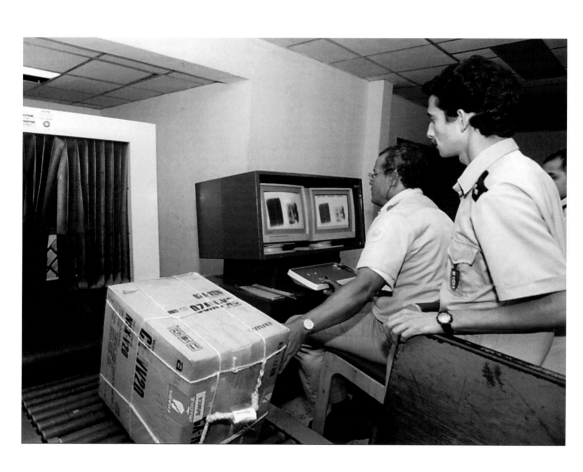

In this photograph, two security employees at Havana, Cuba José Marti Airport inspect packages from South America. Although Cuba has increased trade with South American countries since the demise of Communism in the former Union of Soviet Socialist Republics (U.S.S.R.) and Eastern Bloc nations, this increased trade has also exposed Cuba to the threat of increased drug trade.

CHAPTER 6

The Federal Aviation Administration Today

SINCE THE CREATION of the FAA, many high-priority issues ranging from drug smuggling to hijacking have plagued the aviation community. In turn, the FAA has continued to issue new regulations and safety standards in its primary effort to promote air safety. In addition to performing regulatory functions, the FAA delegates the following responsibilities to its staff of over 48,000 employees: air traffic control and approval of flight plans, airport safety, researching and controlling noise pollution research and control, terrorism prevention, and weather data reporting.

From agency headquarters in southwest Washington, D.C., the administrator directs the FAA—the largest administration in the Department of Transportation—with the help of a deputy administrator. Fifteen associate administrators, responsible for directing organizations and programs related to the agency's principle functions, report to the administrator. In turn, the administrator reports to the secretary and deputy secretary of the Department of Transportation.

In addition to its main headquarters, the FAA comprises nine regional locations throughout the country and two major centers, the Mike Monroney Aeronautical Center in Oklahoma City, Oklahoma, and the William J. Hughes Technical Center in Atlantic City, New Jersey. Currently, the FAA controls air traffic at more than 350 airport traffic control towers, where controllers provide instructions for the take-off and landing of aircraft. In addition, the FAA operates 22 air route traffic control centers throughout the country that guide aircraft along pre-approved flight routes. In total, the FAA operates more than 32,500 different air navigation and air traffic control systems, including radar and automated flight service stations.

Air Traffic Control

The FAA follows a standardized system of air traffic control developed by the International Civil Aviation Organization in the 1950s. The organization's standards include the use of English as the universal language of the skies (due to the fact that the United States pioneered the development of aircraft navigation systems and radio communications) and the use of **VOR** (very-high-frequency omnidirectional range) and satellite systems as the primary navigation tools.

In the United States, air traffic controllers are responsible for maintaining more than 200,000 takeoffs and landings every day, totaling more than 73 million per year. Air traffic control is essentially a combination of three elements: the basic set of flying rules that pilots follow in the air; the use of electronic navigation systems and instruments that pilots use to remain on course; air traffic controllers and the computer systems they use to track aircraft during take-off, flight, and landing.

The basic system of air traffic control relies on pilots providing their own navigation in order to visually avoid other aircraft. Under this system, known as Visual Flight Rules (VFR), pilots navigate using charts that display terrain features, airports, and landmarks. Radio beacons and other ground-based navigational aids can also be used. Pilots using visual flight rules must fly at specified altitudes reserved for their

The largest air traffic control tower ever built by the FAA was dedicated on October 10, 1996 at Chicago's O'Hare Field. The former tower was constructed in 1972. The tower boasts state-of-the-art technology, such as the ASDE3 digitized ground radar system, shown here.

general direction of flight. Visual flight rules can be used when aircraft speeds are fairly low, air traffic is sparse, and visibility is good. (While the U.S. National Weather Service is responsible for gathering weather data at approximately 250 land stations throughout the United States, approximately 750 supplementary data-gathering stations are maintained by other agencies, such as the FAA.)

When any of the visual flight rules conditions cannot be met, pilots must operate using Instrument Flight Rules (IFR), a more complex set of flight rules. Although airlines and larger aircraft almost always operate under instrument flight rules, the FAA requires that all aircraft use instrument flight rules when flying near major metropolitan areas or at the high altitudes normally used by commercial airliners. Pilots flying under instrument flight rules must have an instrument pilot certificate, must file a flight plan before take-off, and must wait for clearance from air traffic control before departing. The pilot must also maintain radio contact with air traffic controllers throughout the flight.

The FAA also operates 95 flight service stations, many of which are automated. In addition to providing weather briefings and flight planning information to pilots, they record flight plans from pilots, provide in-flight assistance to VFR aircraft, and coordinate search and rescue operations.

Noise Pollution

After increased pressure from public interest groups like Friends of the Earth and Sierra Club in the late 1960s, the government passed a law in 1968 that gave the administrator of the FAA the authority to set noise limitations for new aircraft. As a result of the law, the FAA also began exploring and ordering equipment that would reduce the noise of existing aircraft. The agency now requires that new aircraft meet specified noise standards and that old aircraft be retrofitted or retired. In the 1970s, supersonic transports were the subject of much debate over the sonic boom they created and are now required to fly over U.S. territory at subsonic speeds.

In addition, the FAA must approve aircraft noise plans and conduct environmental impact studies before local authorities can receive funding to expand or develop new airports. With FAA approval, local airport authorities have been able to reduce the impacts of noise pollution by routing flights over water or unpopulated areas and by limiting traffic at night. The FAA also encourages airport officials to take additional steps, such as constructing sound barriers, insulating buildings, and restricting residential development in noisy areas.

Airport Safety

Since 1973, the FAA has required airports to provide security measures such as baggage screening and passenger photo identification. However, in the wake of the September 11 attacks, the FAA has imposed stricter safety regulations. After the attacks, the American public was amazed to learn how lax airport security had become. In addition to outdated metal detectors and x-ray machines, security personnel were severely underpaid and undertrained and received no criminal background checks. As a result, the FAA began conducting background checks on all 75,000 employees with access to security checkpoints and asked airlines to check their passenger list against the FBI's lists. In addition, Congress voted to federalize airport baggage screeners, resulting in better training and increased pay for those workers.

Future of the FAA

The FAA plans to meet the following long-term goals by 2007:

> . . . reduce U.S. aviation fatal accident rates by 80 percent from 1996 levels; prevent security incidents in the aviation system; and provide an aerospace transportation system that meets the needs of users and is efficient in the application of FAA and aerospace resources.

Toward that end, the FAA is currently embarking on a major project to modernize the air traffic control system. In fact, two new systems have already been developed and are planned for installation by the FAA. In the near future, the FAA is planning for all communication, navigation, and air traffic surveillance to be handled by satellites, which provide a better system of area navigation than ground-based radio stations. In fact, satellite systems are so accurate that even the International Civil Aviation Organization has agreed to make satellite navigation the standard for international aviation navigation in the near future. In fact, two systems have already been developed and are planned for installation by the FAA

Satellite-based navigation began in the 1980s, when the U.S. Department of Defense developed a system known as the Global Positioning System (GPS). Although satellite

The future of the FAA lies in satellite-based navigation, which began in the 1980s with the advent of Global Positioning System (GPS) technology. Satellites have proven better providers of communication, navigation, and air traffic control than older, ground-based radio stations. In this photograph, the Spartan solar observation satellite is released from the space shuttle Columbia on November 21, 1997. Unfortunately, that particular satellite had to be retrieved afterward due to technical difficulties.

Jane Garvey, the present FAA administrator, at her nomination hearing on June 24, 1997. Garvey noted after the September 11, 2001 attacks on the World Trade Center and Pentagon that "aviation is too important to our nation, our economy, and our way of life."

navigation is well suited for in-flight navigation, it is not yet prepared to guide aircraft during the more complex landing procedure. However, the proposed new system, known as "free flight," will be capable of monitoring each aircraft and alerting the pilot and controller to any possible conflicts. In addition, pilots will be able to personally select and modify their own routes and altitudes. The free flight method is planned to become the standard form of air traffic control in the United States by the year 2010.

Despite all the technological progress led by the FAA, the airlines have seen a significant drop in the amount of people flying. While the airlines compete to stay afloat, the FAA moves forward to reassure the American public of safer skies. As in the past when the aviation industry has seen periods of growth and decline, the FAA is working hard to promote balance within the industry. The FAA hopes that Americans will act as they have previously in the face of airline disasters will not lose their faith in the symbol of American mobility—the airplane.

After all, as FAA administrator Jane Garvey noted in a speech she made after the September 11th attacks, "From the days of Charles Lindbergh, who saw aviation as part of the continuum of human endeavor, Americans have recognized aviation's enormous potential for fostering economic growth and prosperity, for enriching our lives. Aviation is too important to our nation, our economy, and our way of life."

Chronology

1903   Brothers Orville and Wilbur Wright make first successful powered flight

1914   World War I begins

1917   U.S. armed forces enter World War I

1918   World War I ends; U.S. Post Office Department experiments with airmail route

1919   U.S. Post Office Department establishes transcontinental airmail routes

1920   First international passenger service

1925   Congress passes Kelly Air Mail Act

1926   President Coolidge signs Air Commerce Act

1927   Charles Lindbergh is the first pilot to fly across the Atlantic Ocean alone

1929   Great Depression begins

1930   Coast-to-coast passenger service

1932   Amelia Earhart is the first female pilot to fly across the Atlantic Ocean alone

1935   Senator Cutting from New Mexico dies in airplane crash; Congress investigates

1938   Congress passes Civil Aeronautics Act; Civil Aviation Authority created

1939   World War II begins in Europe

1940   Civil Aeronautics Board joins Civil Aviation Authority

1945   World War II ends

1946   United States breaks sound barrier in rocket-powered aircraft

1958   Federal Aviation Act passed; Federal Aviation Agency created

1959   Around-the-world jet passenger service begins

1967   Federal Aviation Administration created

1978   Airline Deregulation Act passed

1981   PATCO strike

1988   Pan Am Flight 103 explodes over Lockerbie, Scotland

1996   Valujet crash in the Florida Everglades

2001   Terrorists steer U.S. airplanes into World Trade Center towers and the Pentagon building and cause crash in Pennsylvania

Glossary

aerodynamic—relating to the motion of air.

aeromedical—relating to the branch of medicine that deals with diseases and disturbances that arise from flying.

aeronautics—the art or science that deals with the flight and operation of heavier-than-air craft.

ace—a combat pilot who has brought down at least five enemy planes.

airworthiness—condition of an aircraft that it is fit for operation in the air.

altitude—the vertical elevation of an object above a surface, such as land or sea.

air traffic control—the process of regulating the flow of air traffic through the use of radar and computers.

Aviation Trust Fund—created in 1970 with the passing of the Airport and Airway Development Act. Receives the vast majority of its funding from a percentage tax on domestic airline tickets and a flight segment tax.

barnstorming—traveling aerial exhibitions that included sight-seeing passenger tours and stunt flying, such as wing walking and plane-to-plane transfers.

Boeing 747—the world's first and largest jumbo jet, with a wingspan of almost 200 feet and a length of more than 230 feet and capable of carrying up to 550 passengers. The Boeing Company has been producing aircraft since 1917.

cargo—goods or merchandise carried by a ship, airplane, or vehicle.

civil aviation—the use of aircraft by private pilots for recreation or business. Also known as general aviation.

cockpit—the frontal compartment in which the pilot and/or co-pilot steer the aircraft.

commercial aviation—The use of aircraft for the transport of passengers, cargo or mail.

Glossary

common carriers—government-certified companies that offer cargo and passenger services to the public.

deregulation—the removal of legal and governmental restrictions on the operation of certain businesses, including the commercial aviation industry.

dirigibles—gas-filled airships originating in Germany early in the 20th century.

federal air marshals—specially trained individuals randomly assigned to domestic and international flights to combat aircraft sabotage.

Great Depression—economic crisis in the United Stated, which began in 1929 with stock market crash and continued through the 1930s.

hijacking—the act of seizing a flying aircraft, usually by forcing the pilot at gunpoint to divert the aircraft to a specified location.

lockdown—a halt of flights from all airports or a cessation of all activity in any other facility.

military aviation—the use of aircraft by the armed forces for military purposes.

radar—a system that uses radio transmissions to determine the distance of clouds, surface features on land and other aircraft.

reconnaissance—a military survey of enemy territory and activities.

supersonic transport—an airliner designed to fly faster than the speed of sound.

United Nations—international organization of countries created to promote world peace and cooperation. Founded in 1945 after the end of World War II.

VOR—radio antennas on the ground that broadcast navigation to aircraft in all directions.

World War I—war between the Allied Powers (Russia, France, Great Britain and later, the United States) and the Central Powers (Germany, Austria-Hungary and Turkey) that lasted from 1914 to 1918.

Glossary

World War II—war between the Axis (Germany, Italy and Japan), and the Allies (Britain, Soviet Union and the United States) that lasted from 1939 to1945.

Abbreviations

ATA—Air Transport Auxiliary

CAA—Civil Aeronautics Authority

CAB—Civil Aeronautics Board

DOT—Department of Transportation

FAA—Federal Aviation Administration

GPS—Global Positioning System

Great Depression—an economic crisis in the United States beginning with the stock market crash of 1929

ICAO—International Civil Aviation Organization

IFR—instrument flight rules

NASA—National Aeronautics and Space Administration

NATCA—National Air Traffic Controllers Association

NTSB—National Transportation Safety Board

PATCO—Professional Air Traffic Controllers Organization

VFR—visual flight rules

VOR—very-high-frequency omnidirectional range

WASPs—U.S. Women's Airforce Service Pilots

Further Reading

Burnham, Frank. *Cleared to Land! The FAA Story.* Fallbrook, CA: Aero Publishers, 1977.

Chadwick, Roxanne. *Amelia Earhart: Aviation Pioneer.* Minneapolis: Lerner Publications Co., 1987.

Christy, Joe and LeRoy Cooke. *American Aviation: An Illustrated History.* Blue Ridge Summit, PA: AERO/McGraw-Hill, 1993.

Haskins, Jim. *Black Eagles: African Americans in Aviation.* New York: Scholastic Inc., 1995.

Parker, Steve. *What's Inside Airplanes?* New York: P. Bedrick Books, 1995.

Pasternak, Ceel and Linda Thornburg. *Cool Careers for Girls in Air and Space.* Manassas Park, VA: Impact Publications, 2000.

Rosenbaum, Robert A. *Best Book of True Aviation Stories.* Garden City, NY: Doubleday, 1967.

Shay, Arthur. *What It's Like to Be a Pilot.* Chicago: Reilly & Lee Books, 1971.

Sullivan, Frank D. *100 Planes, 100 Years: The First Century of Aviation.* New York: Smithmark Publishers, 1998.

FAA website: *http://www.faa.gov.*

Bibliography

Burkhardt, Robert. *The Federal Aviation Administration*. New York: Praeger, 1967.

Burnham, Frank. *Cleared to Land! The FAA Story*. Fallbrook, CA: Aero Publishers, 1977.

Gleick, Elizabeth. "Can We Ever Trust the FAA?" *Time Magazine*, July 1, 1996.

Horton, Madelyn. *World Disasters: The Lockerbie Airline Crash*. San Diego, CA: Lucent Books, 1991.

Kelly, Jr., Charles J. *The Sky's the Limit: The History of the Airlines*. New York: Coward-McCann, Inc., 1963.

Lopez, David S. *Aviation: A Smithsonian Guide*. New York: Macmillan, 1995.

Microsoft Encarta Encyclopedia 2000. "Aviation." Microsoft Corporation, 1999.

Schiavo, Mary. *Flying Blind, Flying Safe*. New York: Avon Books, 1997.

FAA website: *http://www.faa.gov*

Index

ABOUT THE AUTHOR: Andrea Canavan graduated from Syracuse University with a bachelor's degree in journalism. Canavan currently works as a teacher at the middle-school level and spends her weekends working with survivors of domestic abuse. This is her first book for Chelsea House Publishers.

SENIOR CONSULTING EDITOR: Arthur M. Schlesinger, jr. is the leading American historian of our time. He won the Pulitzer Prize for his book *The Age of Jackson* (1945) and again for *A Thousand Days* (1965). This chronicle of the Kennedy Administration also won a National Book Award. Professor Schlesinger is the Albert Schweitzer Professor of the Humanities at the City University of New York and has been involved in several other Chelsea House projects, including the REVOLUTIONARY WAR LEADERS and COLONIAL LEADERS series.

Picture Credits

page

8: Associated Press, AP	28: Associated Press, AP	47: Associated Press, AP
13: Associated Press, AP	33: Hulton Archive by	50: Canadian Press
14: Associated Press, AP	Getty Images	53: Associated Press, AP
17: Associated Press, ABC	34: Associated Press, U.S.	55: Associated Press,
18: Hulton Archive by	Marine Corps	NASA TV
Getty Images	36: Associated Press, AP	56: Associated Press, AP
22: © Corbis	40: Associated Press, AP	
24: Associated Press, AP	41: Associated Press, AP	
27: Associated Press,	43: Associated Press, AP	
Times-Standard	44: Associated Press, AP	

Cover: Associated Press, AP